W9-BLH-604

R01028 6589

ORIOLE PARK BRANCH
7454 W. BALMORAL AVE.
CHICAGO, IL. 60656

DISCARD

JUV
QE
534.2
.W355
1996

Walker, Sally M.

Earthquakes.

$19.95

ORIOLE PARK BRANCH
DATE DUE

MAR 3 2003			
APR 2 1 2003			
JUN 0 2 2003			
AUG 1 8 2003			
JUN 2 5 2004			
DEC 1 5 2004			

DEMCO 38-296

Earthquakes

A Carolrhoda Earth Watch Book

by Sally M. Walker

Carolrhoda Books, Inc./Minneapolis

*For Jean Getzel and Carl Tomlinson, who believe
books are treasures that belong in the hands of
children; and also for Roseann Feldmann, who
teaches the equation:* Science + Children = Fun.

The author thanks Dr. Philip J. Carpenter and Dr.
James A. Walker of Northern Illinois University for
their advice and suggestions. Thanks also to Jill
Anderson (an excellent editor) for using her blue
pencil to bring out the best.

Text copyright © 1996 by Sally M. Walker
Illustrations copyright © 1996 by Carolrhoda Books, Inc.

Carolrhoda Books, Inc. c/o The Lerner Group
241 First Avenue North, Minneapolis, MN 55401

All rights reserved. International copyright secured. No part of
this book may be reproduced, stored in a retrieval system, or
transmitted in any form or by any means, electronic,
mechanical, photocopying, recording, or otherwise, without the
prior written permission of Carolrhoda Books, Inc., except for
the inclusion of brief quotations in an acknowledged review.

LIBRARY OF CONGRESS CATALOGING-IN-PUBLICATION DATA
Walker, Sally M.
  Earthquakes / by Sally M. Walker
     p. cm.
  "A Carolrhoda earth watch book."
  Includes index.
  ISBN 0-87614-888-7
  1. Earthquakes—Juvenile literature. [1. Earthquakes.] I. Title.
QE534.2.W355 1996
551.2'2—dc20
                                      94-36178
                                        CIP
                                        AC

Manufactured in the United States of America
1 2 3 4 5 6 – JR – 01 00 99 98 97 96

The walls of this parking ramp folded during the January 1994 quake in Northridge, California.

R01028 47556

CHICAGO PUBLIC LIBRARY
OLE PARK BRANCH
N. OKETO   60656

DISCARD

CONTENTS

"I was sleeping in a room on the third floor of the hotel when the first shock occurred. . . . I woke to the groaning of timbers, the grinding, creaking, and roaring. Plastering and wall decorations fell. The sensation was as though the buildings were stretching and writhing like a snake."

Dr. Ernest W. Fleming was visiting San Francisco, California, when the Great San Francisco Earthquake occurred shortly after five o'clock in the morning, April 18, 1906. Buildings crumbled into pieces, and broken gas pipes started fires that raged throughout many of San Francisco's wooden buildings. For the next three days, the city was a smoky nightmare.

Although we can't feel it, the earth is always squeezing, pushing, and pulling beneath our feet. Forces inside the earth and on its surface slowly bend, twist, and turn rock. But the brittle rock on or near the earth's surface—called the **lithosphere**—can only bend so much. When the forces become greater than the rock can stand, it cracks.

Sometimes the rock along the crack moves. If the rock moves only a small amount, people may not notice that anything has happened. Sometimes people may feel the ground or the floor shake slightly. Other times, when the rock moves a lot, people may be thrown to the ground, bridges may snap in half, and buildings may collapse. Then the news is reported worldwide: Earthquake!

WHERE DO EARTHQUAKES OCCUR?

No area is totally safe from earthquakes. However, some areas are much more likely to experience earthquakes than others. The earth's lithosphere is made up of over ten large pieces, or **plates.** These plates drift on top of the **asthenosphere,** a layer of rock that is plastic, or able to bend without breaking.

Most earthquakes occur along plate edges, where the plates drift apart, bump into, or scrape against each other. For example, the Pacific Plate, which "floats" in a northwestward direction, scrapes past the North American Plate at a speed of about 1.4 inches (3.5 cm) per year—about the same rate as a fingernail grows.

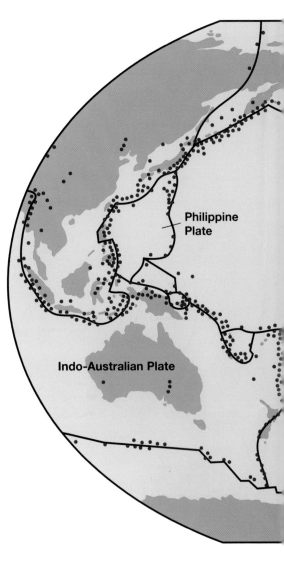

Philippine Plate

Indo-Australian Plate

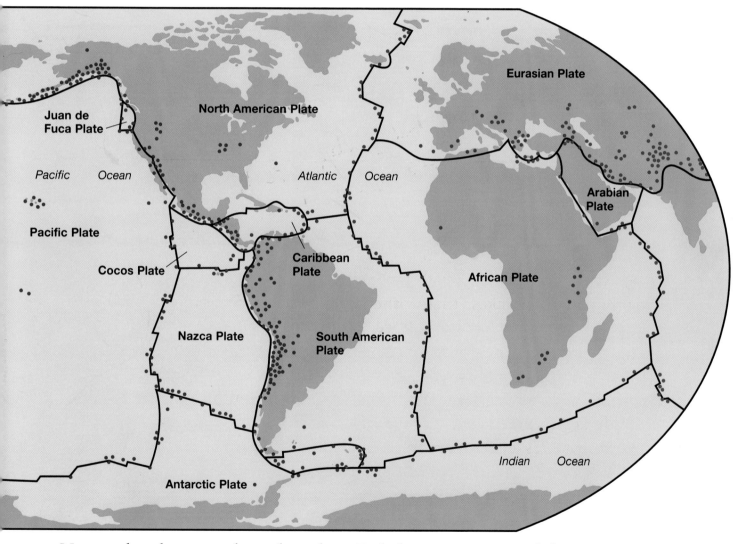

Most earthquakes occur along plate edges. Each dot on the map stands for an earthquake that occurred within the past 30 years.

Left: *As the two sides of a crack move in opposite directions, the rock is strained more and more until one side jerks loose and skips ahead. This sudden motion is what causes the earth to shake.*
Above: *Over millions of years, stress has twisted and folded rock in the Sierra Nevada.*

Plate movement puts **stress,** or pressure, on the edges of a plate, stretching and squeezing the rock into new shapes and making deep cracks in it. This change in shape is called **strain.**

As the rock is strained, energy gradually builds up inside it. When the rock along a crack is strained too much, one side jerks loose from the other and snaps back into its original position, as if the rock were a rubber band that was stretched and then let go. When the rock snaps loose, the energy in it is released, making the ground shake under our feet.

In 1811, the first of several earthquakes surprised and frightened people living near New Madrid, Missouri.

Occasionally earthquakes occur away from plate edges. Three violent earthquakes—on December 16, 1811; January 23, 1812; and February 7, 1812—rocked the ground near New Madrid, Missouri, which is located right in the middle of the North American Plate. People as far away as Boston, Massachusetts, felt the vibrations. It's likely these three quakes were even stronger than the 1906 San Francisco earthquake.

Geologists, scientists who study the earth, believe earthquakes that occur far from plate edges happen in areas where the lithosphere was cracked long ago—perhaps tens or even hundreds of millions of years earlier—by forces that stretched and twisted the rock and then stopped. In places like New Madrid, many layers of sediment, or grains of rock and soil, have built up on top of the lithosphere. Perhaps the added weight of the sediment put enough stress on the rock beneath New Madrid to make it break, producing the three earthquakes.

FAULTS

Once the rock along a crack has moved, the crack earns a special name: **fault.** All earthquakes are caused when rock moves along a fault. Soil covers most of these cracks, so you can't see them. But you may see them in the walls of rock quarries or in sections of rock that have been cut into during road construction.

There are three main types of faults. The first two, **normal faults** and **reverse faults,** cut diagonally through rock. At a normal fault, the rock on either side of the crack is being pulled apart. This causes the rock above the fault to slip downward, just as a person might slip down a slide. At a reverse fault, the two sides are being pushed together. The rock above the fault is then pushed upward, as if someone were being pushed up the slide from the bottom.

| Normal fault | Reverse fault | Strike-slip fault |

An earthquake along the San Andreas, a strike-slip fault, moved one part of this fence 16 feet (4.8 m) and left the other part where it was. Movement along the San Andreas causes earthquakes fairly often, making it an active fault. However, most faults are inactive and don't move anymore.

Strike-slip faults, the third type, are not slanted. They run vertically—straight up and down—through rock. Rock on one side of the fault simply slips and scrapes its way past the other side. To help you understand this motion, lay your hands on a table, palms down and thumbs together. Keep your left hand still, and slide your right hand away from your body. The San Andreas Fault, the source of most of California's earthquakes, is a strike-slip fault hundreds of miles long.

A large amount of strain had built up under southern California prior to the 1994 Northridge quake, which caused major damage to the area.

Just because rock along a fault starts to move doesn't mean it just keeps on going. Friction, a force that slows down movement between two touching materials, keeps the rock from moving very fast or very far. In some places along a fault, friction allows rock to creep slowly and continuously, one side grinding against the other side but moving a little bit all the time. Strain doesn't have much of a chance to build up in these places, and few earthquakes occur.

In other places along a fault, friction may stop the rock's movement for short periods of time. But soon stress overcomes the friction, and one side of the fault skips forward. When the rock skips, the area experiences a small earthquake that does not do much damage. People who live near faults with this type of movement come to expect the ground to shake from time to time.

But sometimes friction causes rock on one side of a fault to snag against the other side and lock itself into position for a long time—perhaps tens or even hundreds of years. During this time, if the stress continues, more and more strain occurs and a large amount of energy builds up inside the rock. Conditions are right for the most powerful earthquakes. When the rock finally snaps loose, the sudden jolt produces a large, damaging earthquake. And people never get used to those!

EARTH SHAKE!

Even if you have never experienced an earthquake firsthand, you know that everything gets shaken around. But how can one underground jolt shake the surface of the earth for up to several minutes?

During an earthquake, energy is released in waves from the **focus,** or place beneath the earth's surface where the rock first breaks. Like a pebble dropped into water, these energy waves, called **seismic waves,** spread away from the focus. As the seismic waves spread, they make the ground vibrate. Each of the several kinds of seismic waves makes rock vibrate differently. And just as you would run through chest-deep water more slowly than if you were running on dry ground, seismic waves travel at varying speeds depending on the kind of rock or other material they are passing through.

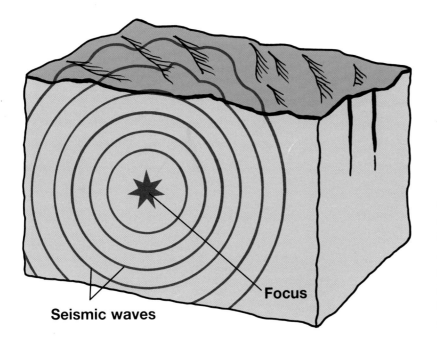

Focus

Seismic waves

An earthquake's focus can be located as deep as 450 miles (720 km) below the earth's surface. However, 75 percent of earthquakes occur within 36 miles (60 km) of the surface. The shallower the focus, the more damage the earthquake causes.

Some seismic waves are called **body waves.** Two types of body waves, **primary waves** and **secondary waves,** leave the earthquake's focus at the same time. Primary waves, or P waves, speed away from the focus at about 2.5 to 4.4 miles per second (4 to 7 km/sec). When P waves pass through a substance—rock or liquid, for example—the tiny particles called **molecules** that make up the substance are squeezed together and then stretched apart. This motion is similar to the way a coiled spring (like a Slinky) moves when it is pushed and pulled across a tabletop.

Primary (P) wave

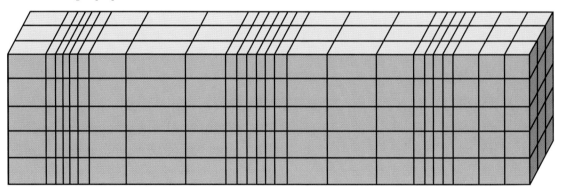

Secondary (S) wave

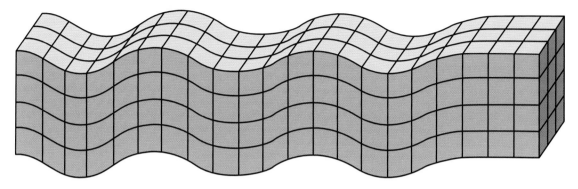

Secondary waves, or S waves, move more slowly—about 1.2 to 3.1 miles per second (2 to 5 km/sec)—and travel only through rock. An S wave moves the way a rope wiggles if you tie one end to a pole and then shake the other end up and down or from side to side. This movement jiggles a rock's tightly packed molecules up and down or back and forth. As the rock's molecules knock against each other, resisting the S wave's attempt to move them, they pass the jiggle along, one to another. After the S wave has passed, the molecules settle back into their original positions.

However, it's curtains for S waves if they reach water. The vibrations stop when S waves reach liquid because molecules in liquid are spaced farther apart and move around more freely than molecules in a solid. Because they are spaced farther apart, molecules in a liquid are less likely to collide with each other. And if they do, they have room to flow to another place. Since there is no resistance, the S wave isn't passed along.

Love wave

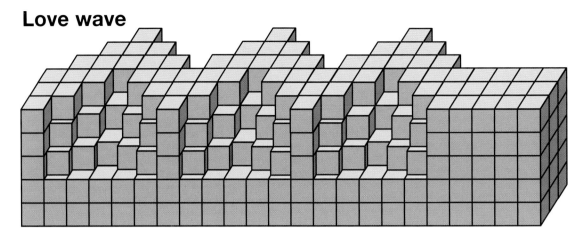

The other seismic waves are called **surface waves.** The two types of surface waves, **Love waves** and **Rayleigh waves,** travel along the earth's surface away from the **epicenter,** the place on the earth's surface directly above the earthquake's focus. Surface waves move more slowly than body waves. They may also last five times longer.

Love waves shake rock particles from side to side as they spread along the earth's surface. Rayleigh waves move rock particles in a circular motion, sometimes making it feel as if the ground were rolling.

Together, S, Love, and Rayleigh waves are responsible for most of the cracked roads, crumbled bridges, and toppled buildings during an earthquake. The sideways movement created by Love waves often does the most damage to buildings, because it can jerk a building's foundation out from under its walls, causing it to collapse. As many as 10,000 people are killed each year as a result of this kind of damage.

Rayleigh wave

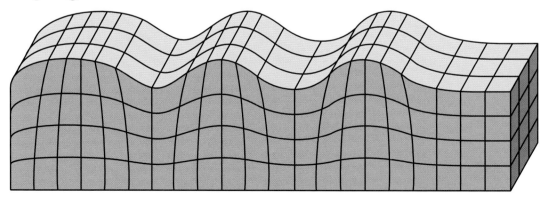

MEASURING AN EARTHQUAKE

Seismologists, geologists who study earthquakes, use scientific instruments called **seismographs** to collect information about ground movement before, during, and after an earthquake. These instruments keep a continuous record of the ground's movement. To provide a complete record of the ground motion during an earthquake, a seismic station must be able to record north-south, east-west, and up-and-down motions.

All seismographs contain several important parts: a weight attached to a wire or spring that senses movement; a device to change seismic waves into a form that can be recorded; and an instrument (often an ink pen) to record the information.

There are two kinds of seismographs: one for measuring horizontal, or side-to-side, motion (left) and one for measuring vertical, or up-and-down, motion (right). A weight (with a pen attached) is hung by a wire or spring so that it tends to stay still, even during an earthquake. But the rest of the seismograph moves when the earth does—including the rotating drum, which holds a roll of paper. As the drum moves, it rubs back and forth on the pen, and the earth's movements are recorded as squiggly lines on the paper.

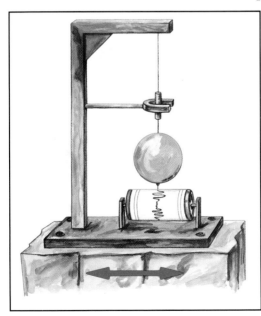

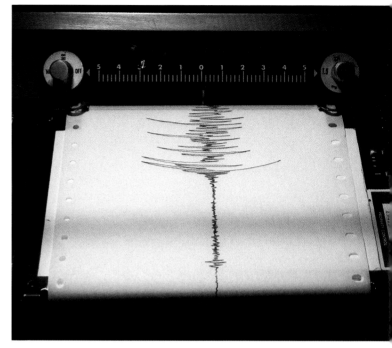

The record of information printed by a seismograph is called a **seismogram.** Seismograms indicate when an earthquake occurred, how long it lasted, when the P, S, Love, and Rayleigh waves reached the seismograph, and how severe the quake was. Seismograms look like wiggly lines. Each "bump" of the wiggly line printed on the paper stands for one seismic wave.

Some advanced seismographs are attached to computers. The computer translates the waves into wiggly lines, and then they appear on the computer's monitor. Other seismographs use electronic instruments to record the earth's vibrations directly onto photographic film paper or onto magnetic tape similar to the tape used in audio cassettes. These recordings are played on instruments that change the vibrations into electronic seismograms or even audio records that let you actually hear earthquake wave sounds.

A traditional seismogram (above), *made by an ink pen, and a computerized seismogram* (below)

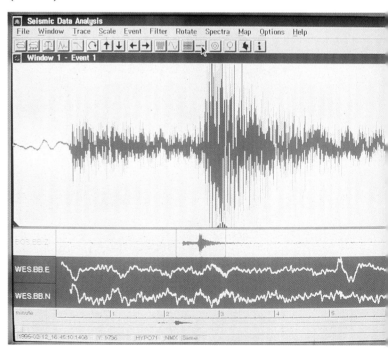

LOCATING AN EPICENTER

As soon as an earthquake is reported, seismologists in seismic laboratories all over the world hurry to compare seismograph readings. Collecting information from several seismographs will help them pinpoint an earthquake's epicenter. This is very important, since the epicenter usually experiences the most damage and people in the area may not be able to telephone for help.

Finding an epicenter requires information from at least three seismic stations. This is because a seismograph can tell us how far away an earthquake's waves began, but not the direction from which they came.

When earthquake waves are received, seismologists at each station examine the seismogram and determine how far away the waves began. Once they know this distance, they locate their seismic station on a map and draw a circle around it that has a radius equal to the distance the waves traveled. When the circles from three or more seismic stations are combined, the circles will meet in only one place—the earthquake's epicenter.

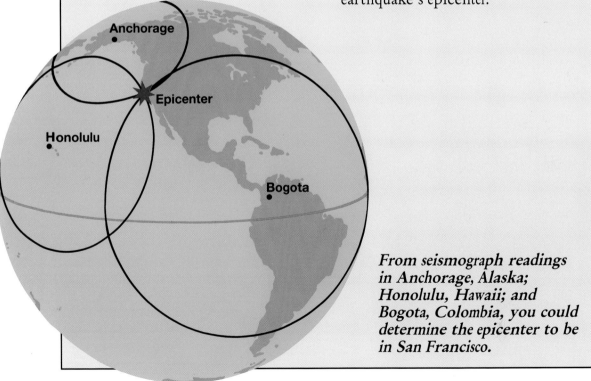

From seismograph readings in Anchorage, Alaska; Honolulu, Hawaii; and Bogota, Colombia, you could determine the epicenter to be in San Francisco.

In addition to the information seismographs provide, it's important to collect observations from people who were there. By keeping records of what people felt during an earthquake and the kinds of damage they saw, geologists can compare earthquakes that occur in different places—those in India with those in Peru, for example. To make these comparisons easier, geologists have developed **intensity** scales. Each intensity number describes ground movement, people's actions, and property damage based on what people saw rather than on scientific instruments. The higher the number, the more severe the earthquake.

Giuseppe Mercalli, an Italian seismologist, developed the **Mercalli scale** in 1902, which for many years was the standard for measuring the intensity of earthquakes. However, in 1931 two American seismologists, H. O. Wood and Frank Neumann, modified the Mercalli scale to take into account more modern construction methods. They also changed some of the examples of damage to make the descriptions more consistent with types of buildings and building materials used in the United States. The updated scale is called simply the modified Mercalli scale. Other countries have since developed their own intensity scales based on their own building methods.

From the damage shown, we can estimate that the 1989 Loma Prieta earthquake measured an intensity of VIII or higher in the city of Santa Cruz, California.

MODIFIED MERCALLI INTENSITY SCALE

I. Not felt

II. Felt indoors by a few people. Some lightweight hanging objects may swing.

III. Felt indoors by more people. Some notice rapid vibrations, as if a large truck were passing by.

IV. Felt indoors by many people and by a few people outdoors. Most people are not very frightened. Dishes and windows rattle, doors may swing.

V. Felt indoors by practically everyone, outdoors by most. Dishes break and windows crack, trees and bushes shake slightly. Small objects move, and some are overturned.

VI. Felt by all, indoors and outdoors. Books, knickknacks, and other objects fall off shelves. Walls crack, and some chimneys break.

VII. Almost everybody runs outdoors. Considerable damage to poorly constructed buildings.

VIII. Difficult to steer cars. Slight damage in specially constructed buildings, great damage in poorly constructed buildings. Heavy furniture is overturned. Walls, chimneys, smokestacks, columns, and statues fall. Water levels in wells change noticeably.

IX. Considerable damage to specially designed buildings. Many buildings partially collapse. Some buildings shift off their foundations. Cracks appear in the ground. Underground pipes break.

X. Some well-built wooden buildings and many concrete, brick, and frame structures are totally destroyed. Ground is badly cracked. Railroad tracks are bent. Landslides on riverbanks and steep slopes.

XI. Few concrete or brick buildings remain standing. Bridges are destroyed. Wide cracks in the ground. Underground pipelines are completely out of service.

XII. Damage total. Waves visible on ground surface. Objects are thrown upward into the air.

Scientists made this intensity map by studying the appearance of the soil and rocks in the New Madrid area and witnesses' written descriptions of the quake.

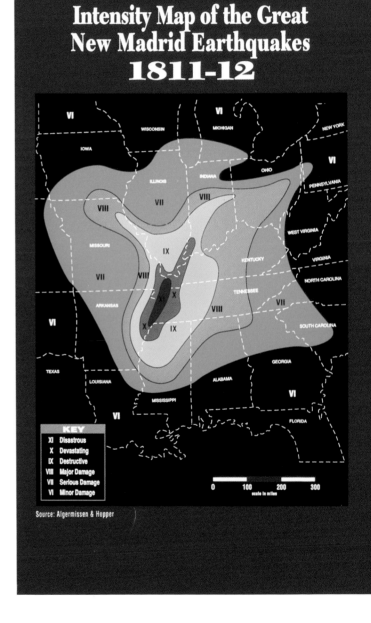

Intensity Map of the Great New Madrid Earthquakes 1811-12

KEY	
XI	Disastrous
X	Devastating
IX	Destructive
VIII	Major Damage
VII	Serious Damage
VI	Minor Damage

Source: Algermissen & Hopper

Gathering eyewitness reports of earthquake damage and assigning an intensity rating is a big job. When an earthquake occurs in the United States, the United States Geological Survey's National Earthquake Information Center, located in Golden, Colorado, steps into action. They mail questionnaires to postmasters, police and fire departments, and to volunteers from the affected area, usually anywhere from 13 to 438 miles (20 to 700 km) from the epicenter, depending on the size of the earthquake. The information gathered from the questionnaires is published every year. Using this data, seismologists can make a map of an area that shows the locations and intensities of earthquakes that have occurred there.

Charles Richter, posing with a set of seismographs. Two of the three drums contain seismographs measuring horizontal movement—north-south and east-west. The other measures vertical movement.

Seismologists also learn about earthquakes by studying the **magnitude,** or measurement of an earthquake's strength. In 1935, Charles F. Richter published a scale called the **Richter scale,** which gives each earthquake a magnitude number based on how much the ground shook. The magnitude number is found by measuring the height of one of the wiggly lines on a seismogram—it may be the line produced by a P, S, Love, or Rayleigh wave—and then plugging that measurement into several mathematical equations. These equations make adjustments for different kinds of seismographs (Richter developed his scale for one special type of seismograph) and for a seismograph's distance from the earthquake's focus.

The magnitude numbers on the Richter scale increase by one number at a time, but the amount of ground movement from one magnitude number to the next is equal to ten times the amount of the earlier number. If you think of the magnitude scale as a very large flight of stairs, standing on the first step could be considered to be an earthquake of magnitude 1. A magnitude 2 would be like climbing up to the tenth step, and a magnitude 3 would be like climbing to the one hundredth step.

The amount of energy released with each magnitude step is even greater than the amount of motion—30 times the energy of the previous number. Again, thinking of a flight of stairs, this means a magnitude 1 would be standing on the first step. A magnitude 2 would be the thirtieth step, and a magnitude 3 would be the nine hundredth step! There is no upper limit to the Richter scale, but the largest quakes recorded on this scale have had a magnitude of about 8.9. Geologists believe earthquakes much above this magnitude are unlikely. It appears that most rock reaches a certain "stretch" limit and snaps (releasing energy) before enough energy builds up for a magnitude 10 earthquake to occur.

Earthquakes Measured by the Richter Scale

Magnitude	Average Number of Earthquakes per Year
1	700,000 or more
2	300,000
3	300,000
4	50,000
5	6,000
6	800
7	120
8	20
8+	1 every 5 to 10 years

The ground shook for almost four minutes during the Great Good Friday Earthquake that devastated Anchorage, Alaska, on March 27, 1964. This tremendous quake, one of the strongest to occur in four hundred years, registered 8.6 on the Richter scale and X to XI on the modified Mercalli scale. Witnesses saw the ground "cracking in big blocks and turning and pulling apart." A housing development on Turnagain Bluff virtually disappeared when the soil beneath it was shaken loose and fifty homes slid down the cliffside.

Cars and houses slid into huge cracks as the soil under Turnagain Bluff gave way during the Great Good Friday Earthquake of 1964.

In recent years geologists have found that for the very biggest earthquakes—such as the Good Friday earthquake—the Richter scale does not measure magnitude very accurately. News reports often still give the Richter scale measurement, but seismologists usually use more precise magnitude scales.

25

The magnitude scale now gaining popularity is called the **moment magnitude scale.** The moment magnitude scale is based on how strong the rock is in the area where the quake occurred, how much the earth's surface area was broken, and how much the rock slipped along the fault. Moment magnitude can be determined from seismograms made by all modern seismographs, as well as by measuring the actual length and depth of the break. Numbers on the moment magnitude scale increase at the same rate as those on the Richter scale.

The moment magnitude scale is more accurate than the Richter scale for measuring very large quakes, because moment magnitude takes into account all seismic waves produced during an earthquake instead of measuring just one. For example, the quake in Anchorage that measured 8.6 on the Richter scale was a 9.2 on the moment magnitude scale. The largest earthquake ever measured on the moment magnitude scale, a 1960 quake in Chile, South America, was 9.5—but only 8.4 on the Richter scale. Unless noted otherwise, the magnitudes given in this book have been measured using the moment magnitude scale.

Over 140,000 people were left homeless by the Kobe, Japan, earthquake in January 1995. On the streets or in shelters, they endured more than 600 aftershocks during the next two days.

IT'S NOT OVER YET

A major earthquake is usually followed by more shaking as rock shifts and settles into a new resting place—just as you may wriggle around in bed to find the most comfortable position before falling asleep. These later tremors, called **aftershocks,** are much smaller than the first earthquake, but they may cause further damage to buildings and roads. Aftershocks may occur anytime from several hours to several months after the quake. At least 42 aftershocks were recorded the weekend of Alaska's Good Friday earthquake.

On January 17, 1995, the lives of people living in or near the city of Kobe, Japan, were shattered by a devastating 6.9 earthquake. Already terrified by the quake, the people of Kobe endured more than 600 small aftershocks during the next 48 hours. Over 5,000 people died as a result of the earthquake and its aftershocks.

Besides aftershocks, earthquakes can trigger several other events. These events, separately and together, may cause as much or more damage than the earthquake itself. Vibrations from an earthquake and its aftershocks can weaken soil and rocks in cliffs, causing a landslide. One of the most devastating landslides ever to occur happened after an earthquake of magnitude 7.8 in Gansu, China, on December 16, 1920. Many of the homes in Gansu had been carved into steep cliffs of very fine, dusty soil. Vibrations shifted the soil, and the cliffs collapsed, killing over 180,000 people inside their homes.

On August 17, 1959, an earthquake near West Yellowstone, Montana, caused a landslide that had a startling effect on the landscape: it created a lake! The earthquake weakened the wall of Madison Canyon, about 19 miles (30 km) west of West Yellowstone along the Madison River. Loose rock tumbled down the side of the canyon, covered the valley bottom, and dammed the Madison River. The huge pile of rock blocked the river and became one of the sides of Earthquake Lake, which is 200 feet (60 m) deep in some places.

Skeletons of drowned trees are a reminder that Earthquake Lake sits where there once was a lush green canyon.

Earthquakes may also cause damage near seacoasts and lakes. The rock and soil in these places are often saturated, or mixed through and through, with water. Saturated soil is weaker than solid ground because water surrounds the grains of soil and keeps them from being tightly packed together. Earthquake vibrations jostle and disturb the saturated soil, and it starts to act like quicksand. This process, called **liquefaction,** occurs in the minutes after an earthquake takes place. Buildings on top of this kind of soil can slip off their foundations and sink several feet into the ground. Sometimes earthquake vibrations squeeze the grains of soil together, and a jet of water and soil squirts up into the air.

Right: Part of this home in Caracas, Venezuela, sunk when the ground beneath it liquefied.
Below: This small cone, called a sand volcano, formed when earthquake vibrations caused a jet of water and sand to "erupt" from saturated soil.

When an earthquake violently shakes the bottom of the sea, the sudden movement may trigger a seismic sea wave, more often called a **tsunami** (tsoo-NAH-me). Tsunami is the Japanese word for "large waves in the harbor." Sometimes people incorrectly call tsunamis "tidal waves," but these large waves have nothing to do with normal ocean tides. A tsunami can travel 469 miles per hour (750 km/hr) and can reach heights of 50 to 100 feet (15 to 30 m) near the shore. Most tsunamis occur in the Pacific Ocean, triggered by the strong earthquakes that occur on the Pacific Plate.

The Seismic Sea Wave Warning System, organized in 1948, helps warn people about approaching tsunamis. When a large earthquake is reported near or underneath the Pacific Ocean, information about the quake and any changes in the water level nearby are immediately sent to the Tsunami Warning Center, based in Honolulu, Hawaii. If the changes indicate tsunamis are forming, a tsunami alert is issued, and people are told to leave coastal areas that are in the tsunamis' path.

The Great Good Friday Earthquake produced tsunamis that pounded Seward, Alaska, grounding boats and destroying property.

In 1960, tsunamis flattened Hilo, Hawaii (above), **then continued on to Honshu and Hokkaido.**

On May 22, 1960, an earthquake of magnitude 9.5 occurred in Chile. Within hours, a tsunami alert was issued for parts of Hawaii, and people were evacuated. The tsunamis crashed onto the Hawaiian shore about 15 hours after the quake occurred, with reports of waves over 33 feet (10 m) high.

Unfortunately, at the time of the Chilean quake, scientists did not realize just how far tsunamis could travel. Seven hours later—more than 22 hours after the quake shook the earth—tsunamis smashed into the Japanese islands of Honshu and Hokkaido. More than 175 people drowned, and entire villages were destroyed by the gigantic waves. Now tsunami alerts are issued over much larger distances so people far across the ocean from the quake's origin can be evacuated.

Since only the largest seafloor and coastal-area earthquakes cause tsunamis, they do not occur frequently. However, people in an area where a tsunami alert has been issued should never be curious and stay to watch the waves. They should leave the area as soon as possible.

A firefighter looks on as flames destroy the Marina district of San Francisco in 1989.

Fires are often one of the devastating effects of earthquakes, landslides, and even tsunamis. Gas and electrical lines burst or snap apart when buildings shift, and fires ignite. About 90 percent of the damage from the 1906 San Francisco quake was caused by fire. News videos of the California earthquakes of 1989 and 1994 contain haunting footage of brilliant orange flames flickering against the black night sky. After the Kobe, Japan, earthquake, fires raced through many traditionally built wooden houses. Thousands of people watched helplessly as their homes became black charred ruins.

HERE IT COMES

It would be wonderful if geologists could issue advance warnings for earthquakes. But reliable predictions are very difficult to make, partly because geologists have not been able to determine a specific pattern of events that leads up to each quake. Many earthquakes seem to strike without warning. This doesn't mean there isn't a pattern—just that we haven't recognized it if one does exist.

		Some Large Earthquakes		
Year	Location	Richter Magnitude	Moment Magnitude	Estimated Deaths
1556	China	unknown	unknown	830,000
1737	India	unknown	unknown	300,000
1811-12	U.S. (Missouri)	7.3–7.8	8.1–8.3	unknown*
1908	Italy	7.5	unknown	120,000
1920	China	8.5	7.8	180,000
1960	Chile	8.4	9.5	5,700
1964	U.S. (Alaska)	8.6	9.2	131
1970	Peru	7.8	7.9	60,000
1976	China	7.6	7.5	>300,000
1994	Bolivia	8.2	unknown	0 (remote area)

*Although we do not know the exact number, records suggest that several people were killed.

Studying the history of a particular fault reveals information that may someday allow seismologists to make a long-term earthquake prediction for the surrounding area. A long-term prediction states a period of years during which an earthquake might occur, as well as a percentage figure for how likely it is that a quake will occur. For example, in 1988 the United States Geological Survey predicted there was at least a 30 percent chance that a moderate to large earthquake would occur in the San Francisco area sometime between 1988 and 2018. That prediction turned out to be correct on October 17, 1989, when the Loma Prieta quake of magnitude 7.0 occurred. Unfortunately, predicting the exact day, month, or even year an earthquake will occur is much more difficult.

Baseball fans sitting down to watch game three of the 1989 World Series may have thought their TVs were going haywire. In fact, they witnessed the first seconds of the Loma Prieta earthquake, which shook Candlestick Park just before the game was scheduled to begin.

A tiltmeter

In addition to studying a fault's history, geologists gather current information from several sources to develop a prediction. They check to see if there has been an increase in seismic activity in the area. About one-fourth of all large earthquakes have **foreshocks,** or small earthquakes that occur any time from several seconds to a few weeks before the large one.

Geologists may use an instrument called a strainmeter, which measures how much the rock along a fault has been bent and twisted by stress. Another instrument called a tiltmeter may be used to measure the tilt and elevation of the rock. But unfortunately geologists do not usually know how much a certain area of rock can stretch or tilt before it breaks.

The information collected about seismic activity, strain, and tilt is important because it helps geologists understand more about the processes that cause earthquakes. However, the information does not really help pinpoint exactly when an earthquake will occur. It is impossible to know if an earthquake is a foreshock until after a larger quake occurs. Likewise, it is impossible to tell if the changes measured by strainmeters and tiltmeters will lead to an earthquake until after it happens.

Some scientists have suggested that the water level inside the ground, in wells, and in streams may change before an earthquake. It may be that seismic activity affects water levels. But water levels can also change for other reasons—such as drought or rainfall.

Scientists are also studying the possibility that changes in animal behavior can signal an upcoming earthquake. People have reported that their dogs, horses, or cattle were restless just before a quake occurred, and in China, photographs have been taken of rats on telephone and power lines, and a rabbit climbing onto a thatched roof. It is possible that animals can sense vibrations we do not notice. But there are many reasons an animal's behavior can change. Unless a change in behavior is observed and reported before an earthquake occurs (most changes are "remembered" by people after the quake has occurred), it won't be helpful in predicting a quake.

People reported rats on telephone wires and rabbits on roofs shortly before the Haicheng earthquake struck China in 1976.

However difficult it may be to predict an earthquake, it has been done several times. One successful prediction was made in China in February 1975. Based on reports of changes in ground and water levels, an increase in the number of small earthquakes, and unusual animal behavior, the governing committee of the Liaoning Province issued an alert that a severe earthquake was likely to occur within the next 24 hours. People were encouraged to remain outdoors, away from their homes and other buildings.

At 7:36 p.m. on February 4, an earthquake of Richter magnitude 7.4 (no moment magnitude reading available) occurred near the city of Haicheng. Many homes were destroyed. Fallen rubble blocked the streets. Bridges and dams cracked and fell apart. But of the nearly 3 million people living in the area, only a few hundred were killed. Had people been inside houses or other buildings, the loss of life would have been horrendous.

The Haicheng prediction was a success and seemed a very encouraging step forward. However, using the same kinds of observations, seismologists have been unable to predict other earthquakes, including the Tangshan earthquake. That quake, measuring 7.5 on the moment magnitude scale (7.6 on the Richter scale), struck China on July 27, 1976, killing more than 300,000 people.

By studying the age of different layers of soil (top), seismologists can construct the earthquake history of an area. They hope that history will reveal patterns of earthquake activity, as it has in Parkfield, California (bottom). Finding these patterns is the first step toward making accurate earthquake predictions.

Seismic gaps, or areas along a fault that haven't experienced earthquakes for many years, may eventually be an important key to making accurate predictions. It's possible the number of years between earthquakes along a seismic gap could help predict when the next quake will happen.

Information from seismographs, other scientific instruments, and historical documents has helped seismologists determine that earthquakes with Richter magnitudes of about 6.0 have occurred along the San Andreas Fault near Parkfield, California, in 1881, 1901, 1922, 1934, and 1966. With the exception of 1934, 20 to 22 years separated the quakes. (Seismologists do not know why the 1934 quake occurred "early.")

Based on this pattern, the United States Geological Survey issued a prediction in 1985 that a Richter magnitude 6 earthquake would occur near Parkfield before 1993. In anticipation of the predicted earthquake, scientists installed instruments to record changes in the ground surface, stress levels in rock, seismic wave activity, and water levels in wells.

The year 1993 came and went, and although a small earthquake occurred, the predicted larger quake did not. The prediction wasn't successful, but seismologists don't think they've wasted their time. They learned a great deal about properly setting up and using many instruments, and they continue to monitor the fault near Parkfield. When the Big One does occur—and it will—they will be ready to collect information that may help answer some earthquake riddles and make future predictions more accurate.

Predicting an earthquake is risky. If a warning were issued, people would panic and try to flee the area all at once. In a crowded city like Tokyo, Japan (left), how could people get out in time, and what would happen if the earthquake never happened?

IT'S SMART TO BE READY

Until we have better ways to predict earthquakes, the smartest thing people can do is be prepared. The old saying "An ounce of prevention is worth a pound of cure" is particularly fitting for people who live in areas prone to earthquakes.

The most obvious way to reduce injuries, deaths, and property damage would be to stop building on or near known faults. Many housing divisions in California actually straddle the San Andreas Fault! But since construction is not likely to stop, scientists and architects are working together to design earthquake-resistant buildings.

The housing development below was built on top of the San Andreas Fault. Inset: In San Francisco, the same fault (left) runs just three miles from the city's airport (far right).

Removing heavy "eyebrows" from the outside of a building (left) *and bolting wooden walls to their concrete foundation* (above) *are two ways of improving earthquake safety.*

Tall buildings are now reinforced with steel and are flexible enough to allow them to sway a bit so they don't collapse so easily. They have fewer decorations, such as concrete statues, that could break off and fall. Houses with wood frames are bolted to concrete foundations so they won't slide off.

Other buildings have been designed to deaden the vibrations earthquakes cause. A movable weight sits on top of each of these buildings. When special motion sensors show that a building is beginning to vibrate, a computer system calculates how much the weight must shift to balance the vibrations and then moves it into position.

The walls of this home in Colombia are being built to crumble into small, harmless pieces during an earthquake. The large roof tiles, however, could still be dangerous to people inside.

In South America, many homes and some public buildings are built of adobe—bricks of sun-dried clay and straw. During an earthquake, adobe buildings fall apart in large chunks, often crushing people inside. Architects have begun to tackle this problem by teaching people to build in a "new" way—which is actually quite old. Hundreds of years ago, South Americans built the walls of their homes by tying wooden poles together in a pattern similar to the strings in a tennis racket. The poles were much lighter than adobe and a more flexible way of supporting walls. Reeds or leaves were woven between the poles to fill the open spaces. Then the whole wall was covered with smooth layers of mud, which hardened like plaster. When this kind of wall shifts during an earthquake, the thin mud layer crumbles into pieces too small to crush a person.

Elevated highways are of particular concern to engineers. When their concrete columns break, the collapsing roadway can injure or kill motorists and crush nearby buildings. But it's sometimes hard to know what will hold up to an earthquake. The elevated Hanshin Expressway in Kobe was designed to withstand a major earthquake. People were stunned when some of its columns snapped and a portion of the roadway flipped onto its side during the 1995 quake. Most of the people killed during the Loma Prieta, California, earthquake in 1989 died when the elevated Nimitz Freeway collapsed. Together, engineers and scientists are working to develop better ways to strengthen and support highways.

Another way to reduce earthquake damage is to connect water, gas, and electric lines with flexible joints to keep pipes from cracking. Broken gas and electric lines can start serious fires that require working water lines to put out. The risk of injury from falling objects can be reduced by installing secure latches on cabinet and closet doors, and not putting heavy objects on high shelves. Ceiling light fixtures should be bolted into wooden crossbeams. High bookcases should be bolted to the wooden supports inside walls.

The toppled Hanshin Expressway

Many people who are injured or killed during an earthquake are hit by falling ceilings or walls. If you are inside when an earthquake occurs, try to get to a doorway. Doorways are reinforced and offer some protection if part of the ceiling falls. If you can't reach a doorway, take cover beneath a sturdy table, chair, or other piece of furniture that will protect you from falling objects. Stay away from windows and mirrors so you won't be cut by glass. Never use an elevator—if electrical lines broke, you could be trapped between floors. After the shaking stops, get out of the building as quickly as possible. Even if the building has survived the earthquake, it may not be safe. After-shocks may make the damage worse.

Many schools in earthquake zones hold drills so students will know what to do during an earthquake. Schoolchildren in this Tokyo school wear padded hats to protect their heads from falling objects.

If you are outside when an earthquake happens, try to stay away from buildings, power lines, bridges, and other objects that could fall and hurt you. If you are in a car, tell the driver to pull over and stop in a safe place. Stay inside the car until the quaking is over. The car should offer some protection from falling objects.

Seismologists study the earth and its movements, trying to learn how, why, and when earthquakes occur. There are many questions for which we still have no answers. Right now we are unable to predict earthquakes accurately, as recent unexpected quakes show. Perhaps as present and future scientists learn more about earthquakes, they will discover new ways to make accurate predictions and reduce the effects earthquakes have on our environment. Only time will tell.

GLOSSARY

aftershock: a small earthquake that occurs days or even months after a larger earthquake

asthenosphere: a layer of bendable rock beneath the brittle outer layer of the earth

body wave: a wave of energy, released during an earthquake, that travels from the focus outward through the earth. There are two kinds of body waves: primary and secondary waves.

epicenter: the place on the earth's surface directly above the focus

fault: a deep crack in the earth, along which rock has moved

focus: the place inside the earth where the rock first breaks during an earthquake

foreshock: a small earthquake that occurs before a larger one in the same area

intensity: a measurement of the movement and damage caused by an earthquake, as felt and seen by people

liquefaction: the process in which water-soaked soil begins to flow like a liquid

lithosphere: the rigid outer layer of the earth

Love wave: a surface wave that shakes the ground from side to side

magnitude: a measurement of the strength of an earthquake based on how much the ground shook

Mercalli scale: a scale developed in 1902 that measures the intensity of an earthquake by the amount of damage it caused and the actions of people who experienced it

molecule: the smallest unit of a substance

moment magnitude scale: a scale for measuring the magnitude, or strength, of an earthquake. It is especially useful for measuring very large earthquakes.

normal fault: a deep, slanted crack in rock, along which rock has slipped downward

plate: one of about ten large pieces of the earth's outermost layer

primary wave: often called a P wave, a body wave that moves throughout the earth in a push-pull motion. It gets its name because it is the first of the seismic waves to reach a seismograph.

Rayleigh wave: a surface wave that moves in a circular motion

reverse fault: a deep, diagonal crack in rock, along which rock has been pushed upward

Richter scale: a scale commonly used to measure the magnitude, or strength, of an earthquake

secondary wave: often called an S wave, a body wave that moves through solid parts of the earth in an up-and-down or side-to-side motion. It gets its name because it is the second of the seismic waves to reach a seismograph.

seismic gap: a section of a fault that has not experienced an earthquake in a long time

seismic wave: an energy wave released during an earthquake

seismogram: a record of ground vibrations detected by a seismograph

seismograph: an instrument used to monitor ground movement

seismologist: a scientist who studies earthquakes

strain: a change in shape or size caused by stress, or pressure

stress: a force that puts pressure on an object, often changing its shape or size

strike-slip fault: a deep, vertical crack in rock where one side slips horizontally past the other side

surface wave: a wave of energy, released during an earthquake, that travels away from the epicenter along the earth's surface. There are two kinds of surface waves: Love and Rayleigh waves.

tsunami: a large sea wave that forms when an earthquake occurs under an ocean, usually the Pacific

A section of the upper deck of the Oakland Bay Bridge collapsed during the Loma Prieta earthquake.

INDEX

Maps and diagrams by John Erste and Darren Erickson. Photographs courtesy of: Reuters / Bettmann, front cover, pp. 27, 43, 44; © Shmuel Thaler, back cover, pp. 1, 12; © Carol Stiver, pp. 2–3; Library of Congress, p. 4; © Eda Rogers, p. 8; Caltech, pp. 9, 36 (both), 40 (right); © Jo-Ann Ordano, p. 11; A. J. Copley / Visuals Unlimited, p. 18 (top); © Tom Pantages, pp. 18 (bottom), 35; © Mary Altier, p. 20; © David Stewart / Gutenberg-Richter, Marble Hill, MO, pp. 22, 29 (bottom); UPI / Bettmann Newsphotos, p. 23; Historical Photograph Collection, #72-152-203, Archives, Alaska and Polar Regions Department, University of Alaska Fairbanks, p. 25; Ron Spomer / Visuals Unlimited, p. 28; National Geophysical Data Center, pp. 29 (top); U.S. Department of the Interior, 30; U.S. Navy, p. 31; UPI / Bettmann, pp. 32, 34; Center for Earthquake Research and Information, p. 38 (top); Jo-Ann Ordano, Photo / Nats, p. 38 (bottom); Minneapolis Public Library, p. 39; NASA, p. 40 (inset); U.S. Geological Survey, pp. 41 (left, #749), 47; California Governor's Office of Emergency Services, Earthquake Program, p. 41 (right); Pat Morrow / CIDA, p. 42; Jerry Boucher, p. 45.